# CAT TRIVIA

**Cartoons**

**© Elliot S. Carruthers**

**© Elliot S. Carruthers 2009-2021**

**ISBN-13:978-1500528034**
**ISBN-10:150052803X**

Kittens will chase bugs but not eat them. The mama cats have to teach them by  eating a bug in front of them. Otherwise... bugs are nothing but a toy.

# CATS HAVE VIDEO SKILLS

## CATS ARE EAGER TO EAT

If you feed your cat dry food... you must give it lots of water. If you feed your cat wet food... it will get about two-thirds of the water it needs.

## CATS LOVE FISH

Cats usually do not capture fish in the wild and they don't like going in the water.

# AILUROPHILE

**An ailurophile is a cat lover.**

An ailurophile is also known as a felinophile. A more common term is a cat fancier. The word comes from the word "ailouros" which means "cat". Ernest Hemingway, the famous writer, was an ailurophile and he owned many cats. Mark Twain was another author who loved cats.

## CATS LOVE A BELLY RUB

Cats may not like a belly rub. If your cat lets you rub its belly... it means it trusts you.

# A FURRY ALARM CLOCK

**Your cat will wake you.**

Don't buy an alarm clock. Don't try
to pull the covers over because
cats are toe attackers. Expect a

few head taps in the morning along with ear meowing. I keep a bag of catnip under the blanket and toss it across the room when a cat tries to wake me.

# Your cat judges you.

A cat owner never trusts someone
their cat does not like. Smart.

Cats know what time you get up.

They will make sure to wake you forty minutes earlier. Cats want you to get up and feed them and to hang out with them. They know you can't fall asleep once you are up. They know the lack of sleep will weaken you to their feline ways.

A good trick is to sleep in the attic.

Pull the stairs up. Remember to bolt the windows and to sleep in a zipped sleeping bag with steel-toed boots. The boots will protect against the attacks and the sleeping bag will hide the location of your head.

# You amuse your cat.

Studies show cats recognize your
voice from another room. They
simply choose to ignore you. They
respond best to a high-pitched
female voice.

# CATS LOVE BEING ALOOF

A challenge to your self-esteem. Don't let it get you down or the cat wins. Get a hobby and do something constructive to occupy your mind. Ignoring you is one of the techniques of a savvy cat. You doubt your very existence.

Call a friend. Get Alexa or a mouse. Open the window and call out to your neighbor. Meditation is an excellent counter. Start to meditate each time your cat ignores you. Fight fire with fire. Your cat has great self-esteem unlike your fragile human ego.

## FERALS ARE WILD.

Feral means the cat is untamed...
often after escaping into the wild.
Feral cats can be tamed with
patience and time.

# CATS LOVE TO AMBUSH

The random attack is impossible to defend. Take a martial art to develop your reflexes. Weave and bob as you walk to throw off their timing. You can't hear them coming so you need to be alert and check your surroundings.

Have a lot of mirrors.

Mirrors will give peace of mind and keep you safe. The surprise attack

will keep you living in a state of
fear. Fight to remember it is way
smaller than you.

**Cats are night hunters.**

You're vulnerable when you sleep.
Take countermeasures. Sleep with
your head where your toes would
go. Get a fake head and put it

where your feet now are. The cat
will walk on the fake head leaving
you to stay asleep under the
covers.

## HAVE FISH... RULE THE CAT.

Fish is high in quality protein. Cats do not eat carbohydrates and they don't need them. They need lots of protein... especially purine.

# CATS CAN APPRAISE

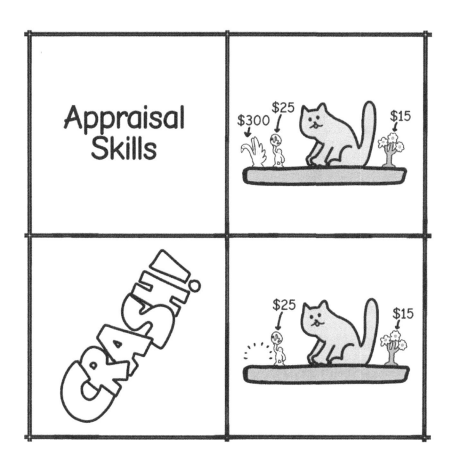

## CATS HATE STORMS

You should microchip your kitten so it can be identified if lost in a storm.

House cats lose their instincts about staying safe and need your protection.

The chip tells anyone who finds them... where they live.

# MATISSE LOVED CATS.

Self-portrait by Fluffy. Circa.
1856

## CATS HAVE A LARGE VOCABULARY

Cats chatter when they see a bird.

Cats purr when they are happy.

Cats hiss when they are mad.

# THE AVERAGE CAT

**The average cat is nine inches tall.**

A cat lives an average of fourteen years and sleeps fifteen hours a day. There are two billion cats in the world. There are 70 million cats in the United States.

CATS WEAR COLLARS AS A
FASHION STATEMENT.

Cats don't wear collars to warn birds. They wear bells to learn how to walk silently.

# YOUR CAT SEES YOU AS A HORSE.

**What to do if a cat jumps on your back.**

Panicking will make the cat panic. There are retracted claws on your back, so don't stand up. Standing up will get you snared. Stay bent over and walk to a counter or table. Tuck your head and the cat will jump off.

**OUTDOOR CATS DON'T GO
FAR FROM HOME**

**Outdoor cats tend to stay near their house and don't travel long distances.**

On average... they only go up to 150 feet from their abode.

# BALANCE

**Cats always land on their feet.**

This is the "Righting Reflex". A cat knows which way is up at all times because of a fluid in the ear canal that acts as a level. A level is a stick that has water in a glass bubble with an air pocket in it. The air bubble will always point straight up so the cat can feel which way is up. The ears also help. The ears let the cat hear the ground much like a bat. The tail also helps with balance by acting as a counterweight much like a tightrope walker's pole.

# Your cat sees your books as little cat beds.

In fact, two cats took turns laying on my laptop while I tried to write this book.

## CATS DON'T NEED BATHS... USUALLY

Cats are one of the cleanest animals.

They groom themselves all the time. The jaguar is an excellent swimmer and ambushes its victims by swimming. Haven't you seen your cat's fascination with a dripping faucet? Don't let them fool you. You are not safe in the bathtub. Keep the bathroom door locked.

Cats will fight to stay
unbathed.

**Cats bathe themselves.**
There may be a time when you
have to bathe them. Clip their nails
because a cat may lash out in
panic. Try to bathe your cat when
it's calm and relaxed.
Put cotton in their ears.
Keep their inner ear dry. Use
shampoo made for cats so it will be

gentle on the eyes. Put candles around the bathtub and keep the lights low. Put on some soothing music and burn a little incense. Keep a few cat magazines around in case they get bored.

## CATS LOVE TO WATCH FISH

If there is one cat in the house...

the fish are safe because you'll

know who to blame.

# CATS HOG THE BED

## BELLY RUB

The ultimate weapon is the soft belly. Every cat knows it's irresistible. Cat bellies induce a trance-state in all who pet it. Be aware of getting trapped. In mid rub, all four paws may clamp down locking your hand in place.

**There's always time for a belly rub.**

Always test the belly first. Get permission. Withdraw your hand if even one claw comes up. Once you can rub the belly, the cat is yours. Keep alert for attitude. Say "Ok… ok… ok…" while you pull your hand back.

**SCAREDY CAT
CAME FROM THE
1948 MERRIE
MELODIES
CARTOON**

A person is called a Scaredy-cat when they are afraid of everything.

# CATS LOVE TO BLOCK YOU

Cats love to get between you and things. Cats love to get between you and anything you're interested in. They have a sixth sense for knowing when you're getting to the best part of a book.

## BOOK BLOCK

## Appear bored.

The cat will think bothering you is a waste of time and will move on to another victim. You can also buy a pocket periscope. Cats will block anything.

# I wonder what my cat thinks about.

Cats have REM sleep like people. REM is the sleep stage where people dream.

So... your cat must be

dreaming.

# CATS LOVE BOXES

Beware of boxes.

They are a perfect hiding spot

because they offer cool shade.

They can lie in wait, and will attack

when disturbed. Inspect boxes

from a distance and never stick

your hand in one.

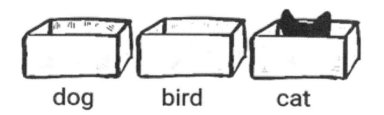

dog      bird      cat

**Wear an oven mitt.**

Mitts are cheap and available. Cats

have "boxopia" which is the belief

they can fit into any size box. "If It Fits I Sits" is a famous meme.

# BOXES ARE MAGIC

# CATS CAN SCARE DOGS

Cats exude confidence and they have troublesome claws. Dogs are too smart to tangle with cats.

# BRISTLES
## Cats have a brush on their tongue.

The tongue looks harmless but it
has razor sharp teeth stronger than
shark skin. The cat pretends it's
only a hairbrush, but it is in fact
very deadly.

## The tongue is like a piranha tongue.

It can lick a dish clean to the bone in seconds. Remember: the cat is always gentle when it licks you to keep you off your guard.

# CATS LOVE BUBBLE WRAP

Distract your cat with gifts.
It will be too busy to plan attacks
on you. Get a cardboard box, a fish
and bubble wrap. Wrap the fish in
the bubble wrap and place it in the
box. Place the box in the middle of
the room and leave. The cat is on
its way, lured by the aroma. Wait in
a safe spot until the popping stops

1. Wrap a fish in bubble wrap.

2. Put it in a cardboard box...

Minutes of fun!

Days of fun!

Someone realized it's great for packing stuff too. The bubbles are the size of a cat's paw and they're perfect for popping. Bubble wrap

fell out of favor with the invention of
the cat laser.

The first cardboard box was a cat
house made for a ginger cat
named Sammy. It is no
coincidence that packages come
with two free cat toys. Do the math.

Your cat likes to lend a paw.

Cats collect stuff. They'll collect

game pieces, wallets, etc.

You'll find them under the bed.

# THE CAT BUTT IS MAGNIFICENT

The cat butt dazzles.

A cat knows you think it's adorable and that's why it puts it in your face. A cat raises its butt to reward you for petting it in the right spot. It knows you love it and wants to share with you.

## THE CUTE CAT BUTT

The butt is perfect for distracting you. It's impossible to ignore. One-eyed wonder cats have starred in a lot of movies. It's comical to see a cat butt peeking out. Of course, it's not so funny when you're trying to finish a good book.

# YOUR CAT IS SMARTER THAN YOU

Research has shown the average cat has the same intelligence as the average two-year-old child.

# CAMOUFLAGE

~ You've never seen a camouflaged cat and you never will.

## Cats are masters of camouflage.

If you are next to a bush or a checkerboard, you can be sure there's an unseen cat there. If you are in the snow and see two dots, run and don't look back. Run when you see glowing eyes in the dark.

Throw everyone behind you as you flee.

### Sock drawers are insidious.

Drawers are perfect for a black and white cat. The invisible beast can lie in wait. Buy pink socks. Put a lock on the drawer and hide the key. The glove drawer is often near the sock drawer so wear a leather glove when seeking a sock. A good pair of goggles is also a good idea.

**Their fur is camouflaged.**

Tiger's fur looks like grass.

Leopard's fur looks like daisies. A

little-known fact is that cats are like

chameleons. The name chameleon is chame-leon or change lion. Cats are where the name chameleon came from. Cats change colors to match their background, making them disappear.

## CATS HATE
## VEGETABLES

Cats have short intestines
designed for moving protein quickly
through their system. Cats need

protein and don't need

carbohydrates.

## CATNIP

Keep the catnip under lock and key. Cats on catnip have gone on rampages and terrorized towns. There are videos of villagers chased by a nip enraged cat. It takes a lot of tranquilizer darts to stop them. Their owners get damage bills and have to keep the cat inside.

**Lock them in a room.**

The proper way to give catnip is to lock them in a room, stand outside and wait for the howling to stop. Your cat will be sleepy at this point.

Keep the noise down **later** because your kitty will be hungover.

## CHORES
**Don't expect a cat to help you clean.**

They want you cleaning so you will come to ground putting your face in pouncing range. A dog will do this for you but dogs take work because they need protection from the cat.

**Cats have no thumbs.**

They will never help you sweep like a monkey. Cats will do one chore a dog will never do. They can give you a kneading massage. The devious feline is trying to learn your weak spots but you might as well

relax and enjoy it.

# THE THREAT IS WORSE THAN THE CLAW

**THE CLAW POSE**

Claws cut everything.

Claws cut wood to hardened steel

before the invention of the knife.

People switched to a rabbit's foot

for luck because the claws shredded clothes.

**Press the pad in the middle of the foot.**

The claws will come out, providing you with hours of entertainment. Believe it or not, cats have killed people with their claws. A cat in Brooklyn lived in a grocery store and attacked a lady shopping there. She sued the store. The lesson is to respect the little tiger.

**Cats have retractable claws.**

The claws only come out when needed. No cat survival book would be complete without discussing the claw. A cat has ten razor-sharp claws. Cats are lightning fast. They are faster than Bruce Lee and almost as fast as a bullet.

# CLAW
# SKILLS

# CLIMB

**Cats get stuck in trees.**

Their downward claws make it easy to climb up trees but hard to climb down. A cat stuck in a tree rescued by the fire department is famous.

## Cats like heights.

Heights keep them safe from predators. Leopards keep their food in trees. The Margay is a small cat living in South America that lives in evergreen trees. Cats love evergreen trees such as Christmas trees and love knocking them over.

Cats are tree climbers. They are descendants of Proailurus, the first cat with claws for climbing trees.

# COLLAR REALITY

**COLLAR REALITY**

What it really says:

I Own
Joe at
41 Prescott St
Garden City
NY

# DEVIOUS

Cats are always thinking ahead.
They're always one step ahead of
you. Like you, they have plans and

schemes. A big mistake is assuming you are smarter than a cat. What would you say about a person who gets free meals, lots of attention and free rent?  Cats are so smart they've convinced you to let them poop in the house and get you to clean it up.

**Cat sounds are devious.**

Meow is me-ow. It means "Me or you get an "ow", it translates to "Serve me or get hurt". Mew is another devious word. Mew is "me" and "new'. Follow my new command. Cats use these words to manipulate you. Did you notice cats can fall asleep in a second and wake up as quick? It is because they're not sleeping. They're only closing their eyes so they can plan and plot.

Cats like sleeping on keyboards. This is so they can take notes and draw maps. Never let your cat have a pen or a pencil to limit their ability to coordinate with other felines. Cats are master chess players and will jump on the chessboard when humans are playing. This is because they can't stand a bad chess player. Cats don't play in

front of you and you won't know
their true skills.

## DOG BED CONTROL

**Don't count on a dog to protect you.**

Dogs are afraid of them too. One look from a cat is enough to turn the fiercest canine into a trembling mess. Their little body exudes ferocity and it's instinctively detected by the bigger animal. Beagles make great cat pals. Boxers and Golden Retrievers like cats too.

**Cats will always outsmart a dog.**

Dogs are very smart but cats are actual geniuses. Think about it. A cat is way smaller than a dog but who is in charge? The cat.

**Protect the dog.**

If you have a cat and a dog… you

must protect the dog at all costs.

The dog is living a life of terror so be extra nice to it.

~ *Cats and dogs do not fight because cats are scary.*

"Fight like cats and dogs" is a myth. Dogs and cats raised together are good friends. It's a myth they always fight. Owning a cat and dog is the perfect combination.  The cat can sit in your lap while the dog can go places with you.

**The cat keeps pests away.**

The dog will keep the burglars away. Cats can mother a puppy and dogs can mother a kitten and they do on occasion. Cats and dogs would be equal if it weren't for one fact… cats are… well… cats.

# EARS

**Cat ears move independently.**

They can move independently in different directions... The independent movement helps with balance. The ear has thirty-two muscles so you can't sneak up on a cat. They can hear a mouse walking and have better hearing than people or dogs.

## Cats are born deaf.

They soon develop great hearing. Thirty muscles help the ear pinpoint where a sound is coming from. Cats can hear five times as far as a human so they'll always hear you coming, which is why it's so hard to sneak up on a cat.

# ELECTRONICS

Cat lovers own the electronic companies.

They made electronics not require thumbs to operate. Coincidence? I don't think so. Why are electronics sold from a "CATalog"? Keep earplugs next to your bed.

## ELECTRONICS KNOWLEDGE

The cat will turn the stereo back on.

They'll put it on after you turn it off. Of course, this is another tactic to keep you from sleeping. Cats like all electronics except vacuum cleaners. The reason is the on/off switch is too high for them to get to and they don't care about cleaning.

## EYES
### Cat's eyes reflect light.

The reflected light lets them see in the dark. Cats love to hunt at dawn. Cats have slit eyes so they can open their pupils wider than we can. This allows for night hunting

and it helps to see on the ground
better.

Never look into the eyes of a cat.
If you look for more than a few
seconds, they can hypnotize you.
You will find yourself going to the
store at three in the morning to get
Tender-Vittles or a bag of catnip.

**Saturday Night Live had a Laser Cat skit.**

In it they pick up a cat and grab it like it's a laser gun. It's funny and the cats don't seem to mind.

# FERAL

**FERAL** (fer-ral)
savage; untamed; undomesticated;

## A feral cat is afraid of people.

# FINICKY
## A finicky cat is exerting its dominance.

Being finicky is to teach you a lesson. The lesson is that you will do anything to please your boss. Images of a starving cat will make you do its bidding. It is not uncommon to walk miles to ensure your friend has its favorite Vittles.

# FINICKY FELINE

## Dedicate a closet for cat food.

A dedicated closet will assure your cat is pleased. Buy every brand and keep it well stocked. The cost is worth the peace of mind. You will not need your umbrella anytime soon.

# FISH

## Cats love to watch fish.

Get a secure tank cover. A motion sensor near the tank can act as an electronic security-guard. Getting a big fish may deter a cat. A bluefish may dampen a kitty's fishing enthusiasm.

## Cats hate water.

Cats love fish, yet they hate the water. The theory is that cats are afraid of the fish, not the water.

They put a goldfish in a swimming pool and the cat would not go near it. They put a whale in a puddle and the cat went crazy trying to get it.  This proved it is the water they are afraid of.

The Fishing Cat loves the water. It has webbed feet and eats fish. It is a cousin of the leopard cat who lives in South Asia. It has spots like a leopard that look like little fish so a fish will think a school of goldfish is approaching.

**The fishing cat does not use a fishing pole.**

Cats prefer nets but no photo of this was ever captured. A pet store sold goldfish and fishing cats. The store went out of business, cause unknown.

# FLOWERS
### Do not count on flowers.

Flowers won't calm the beast. Cats know this trick and will make short work of this. A cat can take a plant down to the nubs in seconds. Their sharp claws are perfect for detaching the flowers. They will wait for you to leave the room so they're not uninterrupted.

**Some flowers are poisonous.**

Don't let your cat eat unfamiliar flowers. You can grow safe catnip in a flower pot. A man in Kentucky had thirty cats so he put down a catnip lawn. He was last seen running down Green Avenue with thirty cats clawing him.

# FOOD

If cats were meant to eat
mice...
...they'd come in cans.

There are no cans in the wild.
House cats don't know how to hunt
so never abandon a house cat in
the wild. Feral cats in your
neighborhood are smart enough to

come to hoomans for food but there are no people in the **woods.** An indoor cat abandoned in the forest has little chance for survival.

## FUR
### The furriest cats are Persians.

Cats with long fur need to have their hair brushed each day or it will tangle and knot.

# FURBALL MINES

## FUR ATTACK

## FUR MARKING

Never wear white if your cat is black.

Never wear black pants if you own a white cat. Cats see opportunities. They are aware of what colors contrast with their fur to maximize marking you.

People are not allergic to cat fur. They are allergic to the dander or dust that comes from the fur. You can get a hairless hypoallergenic cat and you will be sneeze-free. Cats come with short hair and long hair. Long haired cats often need brushing and grooming to stay clean.

**Muscles move their fur.**

A cat's fur will stick up when scared or it feels threatened. The fur will also stand up if it goes near a Tesla coil.

# GANG TACKLING

**GANG TACKLING**

10 PM

11 PM

3 AM

## GREENIES

Feed kittens five times a day.
Feed adults three times a day. It's
a myth that dry food cleans their
teeth. You can buy prescription
food that actually cleans the teeth.
Greenies are a great solution too.

Greenies are good for the gums.
If a cat shows any sign of gum
problems, stop feeding it normal
food and have it eat only Greenies

for a few days. We had a two-year-old rescue cat and the vet said her gums were bad and he needed to remove teeth. A week of Greenies fixed this, and it cured her.

## GUARD
### Cats guard you at night.

Cats sleep with you at night to prevent you from escaping. You can prove this. Get up and go to your kitchen. Like a prison guard, the cat will follow you. It will escort you back and once again take up its position. Cats keep track of us via GPS when we are out. They

want to make sure you don't run
out at night without your cell phone.

# HAIRBALL

### Hairballs look like bugs.

Cats cough up hairballs so you'll
think there's a bug on the floor.
Then you are ripe for the follow-up
trick. They will put a real bug on the
floor. Never pick up a hairball. It
may be a decoy.

# HAIRBALL MINES

The official name of a hairball
is "Bezoar".

# HAT

**Cats do not wear hats.**

Cats don't like dressing up. They will complain and plot their revenge on you. Felines voted The Cat in the Hat as their least favorite book. Dogs love it. Don't make them wear hats. You will pay somehow, someway for dressing up your cat.

## HEAD WALK

# HISS
## The hiss is a warning.

The hiss alerts you to the danger of an angry cat. Keep your hands close to your body.  Have some treats in your pocket so you can toss them and run. Do not own a radiator or a snake since they make hissing sounds too and will confuse you.

## HUNT
### Cats are predators.

Cats don't fear snakes. They are
the ones doing the hunting. Bears
have run from cats. There are
videos called "You Will Not Pass"
that show dogs afraid to walk past
a sitting cat. Even big dogs refuse
to walk by a cat. They both live in

the same house and the cat is the
boss of the hallway.

## Babysitters beware!

There is a video where the cat
thinks the babysitter is hurting the
baby, so the cat attacked her.
Another video shows a boy
attacked by a dog only to have the
cat leap on it and chase it away.

## HYPNO-PERSUASION

## INDOOR OUTDOOR
### Outdoor cats worry about predators.

They have to fight the bad weather and the lack of food. Indoor cats get food, warmth, and love. Caring for an outdoor cat increases its lifespan.

**Indoor cats live longer.**

They live five times longer. Outdoor cats can get frostbite if it gets too cold. Indoor cats are more likely to be obese so make sure they eat right and get exercise.

# INTELLIGENCE

Cats teach horses how to count. Carly the Calculus Cat got her Ph.D. when she was two. She was the first cat to go to Harvard and she invented the automatic pet door. Cats are the smartest of all animals.

**Cats poop in the house.**

They're the only animal that convinced hoomans to let them

pooh inside the house. Further, they outsmart people by getting them to clean up the poop. Dogs were never smart enough to achieve this seat. Cats are so intelligent; they are allowed to walk out the door without a leash. Another feat beyond dogs.

**Cats are as smart as your kid.** Research has shown a cat has the same intelligence as the average two-year-old child. Cats can play chess, create art and compose music, but never do because they don't have to. Dumb dogs have to

chase Frisbees and take on
burglars to earn their keep.

**Cats hide their skills.**
Cats know smarts are not required
so these skills stay secret and
undeveloped. Lions hunt in packs
and use clever tactics. The
lionesses will cause a herd to panic
and run into the arms of a waiting

lion. Lions are terrifying because they're smarter than any human.

**Dear Diary,**
**Today I rode the dog and it made sound a lot. I guess ill give up the spurs. I almost got caught wearing my cowboy hat guess I'll lock the door next time.**
**Hitting the catnip hard but dang makes for good riding**

# meow
# Cat

## INVISIBILITY

# KISS

## Cats avoid kisses.

Cats are very skilled at avoiding kisses. It is impossible to peck a cat who doesn't want to get pecked. The secret is to not make an annoying "meehh" sound when attempting a kiss. Kisses make them think you are sampling them.

It's impossible to kiss a cat.

## KITTEN

Kittens are the cat's secret
weapons.

They're so cute and cuddly they can get away with murder and often do. Kittens are more dangerous than adults because you will underestimate them. Think about it. When was the last time you saw someone scream in a movie because a kitten jumped out?

## KITTEN TRAINING

**Kittens are serial killers.**

A kitten is a small cat which is exactly like saying a small serial killer. The good news is that they can't reach the bed. So stay on your bed when one is around. Kittens are quick learners. Kittens learn their skills from adult cats. Kittens are born with blue eyes and their eye color changes as they grow.

**A group of kittens is a kindle.**

Kittens are born deaf and blind but have a good sense of smell. A kitten will hiss if it smells something unfamiliar. A newborn kitten can purr. Kittens have belly buttons like you. Kittens knead on the mama cat to foster the release of milk.

## KNEAD
**Kneading is not innocent.**

Kneading looks like innocent affection but it has devious intentions. You will have a zillion scratches. It's like the boiling frog- you get it a little at a time. Being a cat lover… the cat will still have its claws because you wanted to avoid the cruelty of removing them. Wear a sweatshirt at all times.

# KNEADING PERCEPTION

# KNICK KNACK

## Do not own knick knacks.

Do not own knickknacks when you own a cat. They allow for target practice. A flying crystal swan makes for a deadly weapon.  There are reports of cat ladies found dead next to a broken crystal swan. I've seen knickknack tossing in action and I can tell you it is terrifying. With practice, they can hit a bug at thirty paces.

## KNOWLEDGE TRANSFER

# Knowledge
# Transfer

# KOKO

**Koko the gorilla had a pet cat.**

The cat lived in the same
enclosure. She chose a grey and

white cat and named it "All Ball".
You can find pictures of Koko and
her kittens at Koko.org.

## LEASH

**Cats don't like leashes.**

Cats don't like leashes and they
don't like to leave familiar territory.
Hoomans don't like to chase cats
when they get off a leash because
they tend to not come back. Don't

use a leash because a cat can slip out. Use a harness or a backpack cat carrier.

**Walk an indoor cat.**

Walk an indoor cat around your property. An indoor cat can get lost because they've never seen their home from the outside. They may not recognize where they live.

# LIKEABLE

# LION

**Lions are sociable.**

Lions are the only cats who live in large social groups. A group of lions is a pride. The males defend the pride while the females hunt for food.

**Cats are little tigers.**

## LITTER

Have one litter box for each cat.
Have an extra litter box. Each box
should have at least two inches of
litter. Cleaning the kitty litter is
dangerous, so be on your guard.
The cat will come flying in when
you finish. The cat can land on you.

Pooh can hit your face. A frenzied feline can cause you to trip and fall. To be safe, buy a self-cleaning litter box and a bomb disposal robot. Get a Roomba and turn it on. The cat will be busy riding the Roomba.

Beaches are giant kitty litter boxes.

Cats bury their poop to avoid predators.

# LITTER KICK

## LOVE

**Cats are fertile.**

In ten years, a cat can be the great-grandma to 700,000 kittens. Cats are superfecund, meaning each kitten in a litter can have a different father. Cats can have their kittens on different days.

Mother cats do a great job.

She will hunt for them and teach them how to hunt. She will stimulate their butts with her tongue to teach them how to pee and poop. Cats can have up to ten teats for feeding kittens.

## LOYALTY

## Cats become upset when you leave.

Get a webcam with a speaker so you can talk to your cat during business meetings. Leave a television or a radio on so they won't feel alone. Leave a picture of yourself on the shelf so your kitty can look at you. Another cat can keep the kitty company and reduce its stress levels.

## Cats can sleep fifteen hours a day.

There's a good chance your cat is napping when you're away. Try not to call the house because you may disturb a good nap. In fact, remove the landline to prevent telemarketers from interrupting a good sleep.

## LOVEY
### Lovey Eyes are impossible to resist.

The eyes will calm you and signal contentment. It will infect you and in return, you will make lovey eyes back. This creates a close bond of warmth. This is okay. It is harmless and your cat won't see you as prey.

**Practice lovey eyes.**

Practice lovey eyes on the people you meet on the street to get good at it. Cats are so smart they know blinking at you can win your heart.

# MARK
**A cat marks with pee.**

It is a way of claiming ownership. Excessive marking warrants a vet visit because it may mean kidney problems. Never leave your clothes out because they may mark it. The theory is the cat is claiming its territory.

## TERRITORY MARKING

**Chemical warfare.**

It may be a form of chemical warfare and cat pee has a time release. You will not be able to smell it on your shirt until you are somewhere out in public. The stink will detonate and get stronger until your eyes water and your nose runs.

## MEOW

Do not underestimate the meow. You will find yourself obeying every command. The meow has many meanings. Cats only meow to their mother or their human. They don't "meow" at each other.

## MEOW OUTSIDE

Cats have a large vocabulary. Meow may mean "feed me", "let me out", "let me in", and so forth. The meow is the least dangerous of all the techniques which is why you will underestimate it. You will begin to understand what each meow means.

People think cats can talk.

# MILK

## Cats can't digest pasteurized milk.

Raw milk and yogurt are healthier for cats. Give milk rarely or you can upset their tummy. Get them a product called Cat-Sip. Cat-Sip is lactose-free milk packed with taurine and a lot of nutrients.

**Cats are lactose intolerant.**

**Don't give them soy milk.**

Soy milk can cause liver and thyroid problems for a cat. Cheese is another no-no.

## MIND CONTROL

You obey your cat.

Did you decide or did you do it because your cat looked at you a certain way or sat in a certain spot? The Egyptians believed cats were Gods. Is there something to that? Are we making decisions or are we cat-controlled robots? You let your cat out. You let your cat in.

## MOUSE SUPPORT

## MURDER
**Cats get away with murder.**

Vampire stories started when cats started living with us. Why do cats hiss to mimic the sound of a snake? To blame the snake. Why are cats attracted to barbecues? They know a barbecue fork makes a good cover story.

## NAP

**Sleeping is passive-aggressive.**
Sleeping is an act of defiance. A

cat can snooze twenty-three and a

half hours a day knowing there is

nothing you can do about it. Even though it loafs and goofs off… it knows you will still feed it and do its bidding. Napping makes you jealous as you go off to work with your cat snoozing

**POWER NAPS**

## NINJA SKILLS

**Cats have Ninja skills.**

The Ninja skills of a cat are incredible. You may not see them but they are always there. Assume you are being watched and you are being stalked. You will not hear them coming because they are invisible when frozen in a pose. The room may look empty but always be on your guard.

# NUB

**The nub is a secret weapon.**

No one knows what the nub does.

It sits on the side of each paw.

Since everything on a cat is deadly, we can only imagine what killing power it has. It may be where the cat stores the breath it steals while you're sleeping.

## OFFSPRING

**Your cat is your child.**

Your cat doesn't know it's not your child. It's best not to say anything because it will become confused and uneasy. Some family secrets are better left unsaid. Love it as your own and it will never know the difference.

**You're adopted.**

**Frame your cat.**

Put photos of your cat around the house. Put bronzed booties on the shelf with their name on it. Always use your best baby voice and use pet names like "baby-waybe".

## OBESITY
### People are the reason cats get fat.

People feed them dry food and they get fat. Dry food is nothing more than cereal. Indoor cats often get no exercise and are more likely to become overweight.  Get an exercise wheel so they can work out every day.

**Don't overfeed your cat.**

They don't know when to stop
eating. An obese cat can get
diabetes much like a hooman.
Overweight cats also get other
weight-related problems. Buy
better food that does not contain
grains or sugar.

# PADS

**The paw was the inspiration for the sneaker.**

The little pads allow a cat to come and go unheard. A million years ago, some cats had clogs on their feet but became extinct due to the clop alerting the prey.

## PADDED FEET

**Don't use rice paper.**

Even rice paper does not alert you.
Cats can no longer become
Shaolin monks because they never
hear the cat coming. An
unexpected mew can upset the
delicate universe. There are giant
cat statues in Japan as a sign of

surrender and admission to the

superiority of felines.

# PESTS

**Cats protect your house.**

A domesticated cat keeps your house free of pests. The Egyptians used them as well. Cats in the outdoors control the rodent population. Rodents would overrun farms without cats. Rodents such as mice and rats carry disease and the fleas on them can carry the plague. Cats are the best rodent hunters in the world. The Black-footed cat kills about fifteen small critters a day. Cats are important in the chain of life.

## Cats do an important job for us.

### Expert pest hunters.

They keep the house free of mice and bugs. People are healthier because of their furry friends. Cats can catch a fly every time. They do this by chasing the fly and waiting for the fly to tire and rest. The cat will then jump and scare the fly, forcing it to start flying again. The bug will fly lower and lower as it gets tired. After repeating this, the fly will be low enough for the cat to grab.

# PET DOOR

**A pet door could be a wise
investment.**

Get a pet door. They actually make
cat doors that open when it detects
a radio chip on your cat. Sorry
raccoons. A twenty-foot python
came through a pet door to eat cat
food and the cat made short work of

him. Don't leave the cat food near the pet door if there are pythons in your neighborhood. If you own a dog too, put a camera inside so it can see the coast is clear.

## PET DOOR SKILLS

Pet Door Skills

## PHONE
**Keep your phone on you.**

Cats have phone skills. Cats use

text messaging to spoof your identity. Keep a security code on your phone. Tofu the cat dialed 911 and saved his owner who was overcome by smoke.

Buy a GPS tracker.

You can buy a GPS tracker your cat can wear. Some trackers allow for two-way communication. If the cat gets lost, you can see where it is anywhere in the world on your smartphone.

## PHONE SKILLS

## POISON

## Never give your cat chocolate.

Keep poison away.
Keep drugs out of reach of your
kitty. Even vitamins can be
dangerous. Never give cat alcohol
or coffee. Keep raisins and grapes
away. Onions, chives, and garlic
are also bad. Toothpaste contains
xylitol. Xylitol is toxic to a cat. It
also comes in sugarless gum and
candy. Never give yeast dough
which is bad. Keep plants away
unless you are sure of their safety.

# POWER NAPS

## POWER STRIP SKILLS

**Cats love power strips.**

They like clicking the on/off button on surge protectors. They like power strips going to televisions and radios. Clicking the power strip allows them to control many devices at one time. Don't bother getting a device to turn your lights on and off. The clicking cat will make burglars think you're home.

POWER STRIP SKILLS

CLICK!

## PRANKS

**Cats are pranksters.**

Many people report turning around to find a cucumber on the floor behind them. This makes them jump. Reportedly no one was home except for the cat and the owner had no cucumbers. Cats can order cucumbers from Amazon.

**Cats have a great sense of humor.**

Cats are behind many practical jokes. They will sneak into a box where you store cables and tie them into knots. They will take your keys and swat them under the oven. They will jump on a board game and make the pieces scatter. They especially like pranking by jumping on chess games, Risk and Scrabble.

## PURR

**Cats can purr at will.**

Purring despite what people think is not involuntary.  It is a tool a cat uses to seduce you. It is the MSG of the feline world. Once a cat starts purring, you can't stop petting it. The melody drones on and it's no coincidence it sounds like "perfect. Cats understand English and have the art of verbal manipulation.

## PURR PET ME

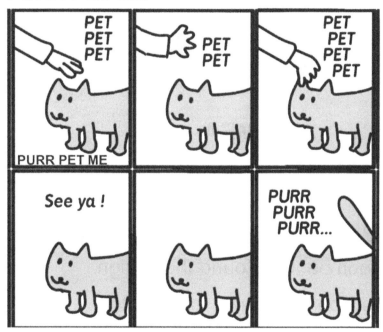

# THE POWER PURR

## ROOMBA

Your cat is a Batman on Patrol.
A lady owning twenty cats invented
the Roomba. She found the design
for the Roomba drawn in kitty litter
on her floor. The Roomba is a
general purpose cat transporter. It
has a cat-sized seat and travels at
the perfect speed for a comfortable

and joyful ride. It allows for easy patrolling.

**Roomba means Room Batman.**

They invented the Roomba as a cat transport vehicle. Someone figured out how to put a vacuum underneath it. People who own cats will buy a Roomba even though they have hardwood floors.

**Cats will ride anything.**

They will ride turtles, horses, and people. It is not uncommon to see a turtle go by with a cat onboard. Farmers can attest their cat rides the horse around the farm. People will walk around with their cat on their shoulder not realizing they are in fact, giving a ride. Toonces the Driving Cat commuted in a Thunderbird for ten years. Look it up and you will find many videos of him driving.

# ROOMBA GETAWAY

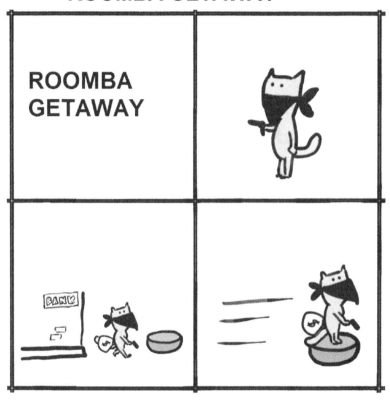

# ROOM BATTLE TANK

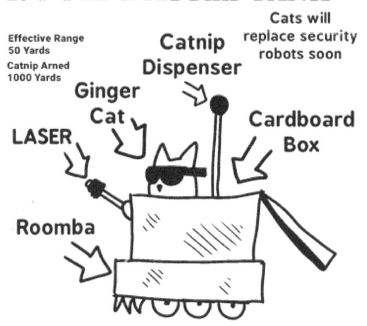

Cats will replace security robots soon

Effective Range
50 Yards

Catnip Arned
1000 Yards

Catnip
Dispenser

Ginger
Cat

LASER

Cardboard
Box

Roomba

# EVERYBODY

# ROOMBA!

**The Roomba is the perfect cat vehicle.**

The wheels and mechanism are hidden to protect the tail. The speed is perfect for a stable and safe ride. The vacuum underneath catches dander and hairballs. The top is one piece of plastic matching the size of any cat. The motor has enough power to carry even the fattest feline.

## SCRATCHING POST

**Buy plenty of scratching posts.**

Scratching in front of you is to teach you what you are up against. Sleep at night with one eye open. Scratching posts are better than declawing your cat. Declawing is the cutting off of the claw at the knuckle. It is painful with possible complications. Cats are easy to train to use scratching posts. Cats missing their claws cannot defend themselves. I know a cat killed by a squirrel because he could not right back.

# SCRUFF

## Grab the scruff.

Grab the scruff to get control of an aggressive cat. The scruff is the loose skin on top right below the head. The mama cat picks up her kittens by the. It will calm the cat because it reminds it of mama kitty. Do not lift an adult cat by the scruff because you could hurt them.

The Scruff

Grab the scruff of the neck to calm them down.

## Gladiators vs. Lions.

A gladiator fought a lion. He grabbed the beast by the scruff of the neck. The mighty feline's muscles relaxed and it purred. Then it ran off with the gladiator's arm.

# SECRETS

## Cats have secrets.

Have you come home and found your browser on a website you did not visit? C is a very popular programming language. "Cat" starts with the letter C.

Coincidence? Why do you think managers say managing programmers is like herding cats? And why do they call programmers hackers? Could it be because cats hack up hairballs? Do the math. Passwords protect your computer and change your password often.

# SECRET SKILLS

# SELFIE SKILLS

## SIDEKICK

**Cats form gangs.**

Cats can get along with other small
animals if they grow up together.
Cats have the ability to align with

them against you. Cats make little gangs with one agenda- you. Remember: when a cat is around, you cannot even trust a hamster. Cats can also make friends with horses and other big animals.

Cats can befriend squirrels.

# SLEEP

## LAP PIN

**Don't allow a cat to sleep in your lap**

You will not want to disturb the sleeping feline. Keep a phone nearby and have fresh water in case the power goes out and you can't use the phone. Help may be

days away.

A sleeping cat trusts you.

Sleeping in your lap means your

cat trusts you. A cat can fall asleep

in one and a half seconds. It takes

two seconds to get up from a chair

so a cat can pin you every time.

## SNORE

**Guard your bed.**

Never give up your position. A cat
will use any means to keep you
exhausted and that includes
depriving you of all sleeping spots.
It is common to step out of a bed
for a mere second only to turn

around and find a snoring cat. It
may be impossible to move it and
you will find yourself dangling off
the bed as you try to sleep.

# SPAY

## Clipped ears.

A catch and release cat has a clipped ear to show it's fixed. Returned to its group, a feral cat can live a much longer life if it has a human caretaker. A cat is "fixed" by undergoing an operation that stops its parts from working.

## A personal decision.

Getting your cat fixed is a personal decision as the cat will never be able to have kittens. If a cat is not fixed she may show up with unwanted kittens that you may have trouble getting homes for. A spayed (fixed) cat will stop going into heat (yowling for males) and you both may live a quieter life.

# STARE AT NOTHING

## Staring is a common trick

The cat stares as if something is there that you can't see. It does it so you believe there must be a ghost or a monster. This is Catlighting. The Death Stare is when the cat stares right in your eyes as if it wants to kill you but realizes you are too big. This is the mask slipping and you get an insight into the little devil. Don't make sudden moves and back out of the room while keeping your eyes glued.

# THE DEATH STARE

**The Surprise.**

The "Surprise!" may be the creepiest of all. You feel watched and turned around to find a cat staring at you. A cat thinks you can't see it when it stays still. It will stay quiet even as you speak to it. It will run away when it realizes you can see it.

## The Stare at Nothing
## Is something there?

The other theory is that something is there. You can't see it and the cat is protecting you from it. In Japan, owning a Calico cat is lucky. Could it be that the cat is keeping away bad spirits? Everyone knows a cat can steal your breath while you sleep, so they can breathe in a ghost as well.

### Time portal theory.

Another theory is that cats are seeing time portals the same way we see an exit ramp on a freeway. Have you ever noticed a cat disappear after a staring session?

## STATIC

### Cats can stun you.

Cats use static electricity to stun their victims. A good shock is a polite way to say it's time to stop petting me. It's also an attempt to make you wet your pants. Some shocks have been severe enough to throw a big man across the room.

## STATIC ELECTRICITY

**Cats have endless power.**

A scientist in Germany used cats to supply power to Hamdorf. Never

walk across a shag rug, then stand
in water and pet a cat. Never use a
cat as a towel. Water is a perfect
conductor.

## STEALTH

Your friend is quiet.
Cats are quiet.

Cats are prey for bigger animals.

Purring shows happiness in a quiet way.

**Cats are crepuscular.**

Crepuscular means they are active around dawn and twilight.

# TABBIES AND CALICOS

Orange tabbies tend to be male.

Most Calico cats are female.

A CALICO TOOK A SEAT,
IN FRONT OF A PICASSO,
I COULD ONLY SEE ITS FEET,
THEY WERE WHITE AS SNOW.

A calico has black and orange patches.

Tabby fur is perfect for the wild. They are common outdoor cats. Calicos are famous for their eclectic colors. It is very rare for a calico to be a male. In fact, 99% of calicos are female. Calicos are famous for their sweet, loving personalities. Calicos have three colors in their fur. White, orange and black.

## TAIL TOY

**The tail is a toy.**

Excessive tail attention may mean fleas. A tail obsession is a good reason to see a vet.  Cats carry many weapons and tools that look innocent.  Don't fall for their harmless facade. The tail allows for balance when chasing you but it is effective for knocking things over. It's great for toppling coffee on a keyboard. It is also the perfect eye blocking tool. The tail comes with a hair trigger so the cat will spin and latch onto you. The tail of a cat has a brain and a mind of its own. The tail is also perfect for ticking your nose.

# TAIL PRIDE

# TAIL ATTACK

# TAIL POP

## TALK

### Conversations with your Cat.

Do you talk with your cat? Of course, you do. This means you're one step closer to being a cat lady. A cat lady can be a man or a woman. Soon you will hear your cat and understand every word.

You will answer. "Meow". "Okay.

I'll get your food."

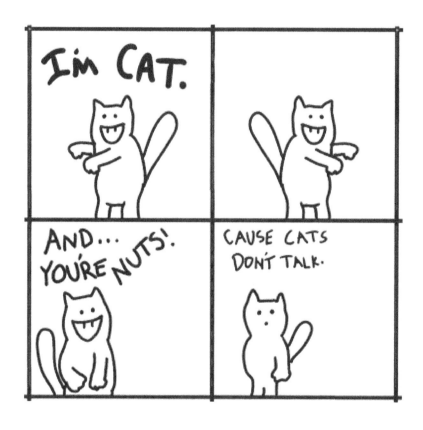

# TEACUP

**Teacup cats are tiny.**

A teacup cat weighs about a third
the weight of a normal cat.
Teacups can fit inside a teacup,

thus the name. Teacups are tiny cats with proportional bodies. They're bred to be small and they are very rare. Teacups hunt in packs and a hundred teacups can take down any animal on the planet.

## TEETH

## Cats can infect you.

Cat bites and scratches can become infected. Cat Scratch Fever comes from cat scratches. It can be serious so you should see a doctor. Kittens have baby teeth and grow 26 needle-like milk teeth. 30 adult teeth replace them at around six months.

# THEFT

## Cats steal food.

Cats love to steal food to deprive you of nourishment. They will often take food having no interest in eating it. If it does make a tasty meal then it is a win-win. The anxiety caused by having to guard your food is an added bonus. I recommend hanging your food high in sacks hoisted on poles. Use motion detectors to alert you to a scavenger.

# THUNDER

**Thunder terrifies cats.**

Rub Bach Rescue Remedy on their fur to calm them during thunderstorms. You can also try a Thunder Shirt. It will give a constant hug to assure them. Stay calm yourself so your cat will stay calm. Make sure there's a safe place for them to hide. Play thunder sounds very low to get your cat used to the sound of thunder. Close all the doors and windows and keep the shades down as well.

## TIME TRAVEL

### Keep your birth secret.

Never let your cat find out where and when you were born. Cats can time travel. How many times are you sure your cat is sleeping next to you only to find it has vanished?

Reappearing seconds later? Don't let a cat travel back in time and get you as a baby. As proof… open a scrapbook and read it. The cat will try to read it too.

# TOES

**Your toes are a target.**

Your toes are a target under a blanket. They will wait for you to fall asleep to launch an attack on your digits. Keep your toes still because wiggling toes look like struggling prey.

# TOE BITE

**Keep your feet still.**

Moving your feet away will not work because it only excites them. The cat will leap and pounce on your retreating tootsies as the chase instinct kicks in. You can also sleep with your shoes on. Keep a cat toy under your blanket. The stick toy with a feather on a string is perfect for this task.

## TOILET PAPER

**Toilet paper will be shredded.**

Stealing your toilet paper is a guerilla tactic designed to wear you down. They know a smelly bum makes for an unhappy hooman and that's what they want. The more they weaken you… the easier it is to take you down. They will shred each piece into unusable shreds. A good preemptive counter is to buy a bidet to use to wash your bum.

## Cats love toilet paper.

Toilet paper was invented as a cat toy and named "Toy-Let" paper or "Let the cat have a toy". Cats learn your bathroom habits and they know the time to take down the toilet paper. My advice is to go into the bathroom and make loud grunting noises so your cat won't know when you go.

# TOILET PAPER TERROR

**Always keep a spare roll.**

Practice using ripped up little shreds. Put the paper on the roll under rather than over. It will be harder for their paws to pull it down. Never buy toilet paper with pictures of bugs, birds or mice as this will double the frequency of T.P. attacks.

Cats T.P. houses.

Cats are good tree climbers and they drag toilet paper into trees so other predators can't get it. They know hanging white strips sends a chill down your spine. This is why they do it on Halloween.

## TOSS

**Cats will toss dead critters.**

Indoor cats toss bugs and the occasional mouse. Outdoor cats will toss birds, mice, and the occasional lizard. Play handball to develop your reflexes so you can slap away the morbid gifts.

## DEAD CRITTER TOSS

DEAD CRITTER TOSS

**The dead critters may be a gift.**

Tossed because your cat loves you. It may be because your cat thinks you don't know how to hunt and it's trying to teach you. Try to catch it with your mouth so your cat

may think you learned how to hunt.

If you think it was given as a gift,

take a few bites and say "Yum!"

# TOYS

**Toys are serious business.**

Young cats practice hunting and older cats stay fit. Toys will make your ankles look less fun. Cats might bite when they don't have enough toys. Toys also calm your cat by expending energy. A great toy is a big wheel the cat can run on. It looks like a giant hamster wheel for cats.

## VACATION

**Cats like vacations.**

A French cat took a vacation on board the spaceship Veronique AGI and was in space for fifteen minutes. She came back safe and sound. In 2002, a cat disappeared while on vacation. They found the cat 140 days later and 350 miles away.

# VEGETABLE

**Cats hate vegetables.**

Vegetables will annoy and piss off
any self-respecting tabby. It's
always a good idea to own a rabbit
if you own a cat. The rabbit will eat
the foliage leftovers the cat is not
interested in. Cats don't have the

right enzymes for digesting
vegetables. They do have a catnip
enzyme. Catnip is the only veggie
they like.

## VELOCITY

Cats can jump five times their
height.

The velocity of a cat is proportional to a hand reaching for a garment.

# VET

**Cats hate the pet carrier.**

The carrier reminds them of the vet. Leave the carrier out and let them play in it so it won't remind them of the vet when the time comes. Practice going on car rides with your cat in the carrier so it will be less fearful. You can buy a pheromone spray to calm your cat. Another option is the Sentry Calming Collar which contains these pheromones. Another option is to have your veterinarian prescribe a sedative. Remember to stay calm and to talk in a soothing voice.

**Videos are cat propaganda.**

They hypnotize people into believing in the cat agenda. Cats know you will be weak from watching videos until five in the morning. You can never watch one. Click on one video and you end up

watching hundreds until you pass
out.

Cat videos get millions of views.

# VIDEO ADDICTION

## WAKE

### Cats torment you when you're sleeping.

This night attack is another effective measure that is impossible to defend against. Cats are experts at spotting weak points and exploiting them. The good news is that cats are small so you can get them out of the room and shut the door. It's only a matter of time until they learn how to open the door.

**Anything exposed will get
tapped.**

Pleading will do no good since they can't speak. Rolling over does not work because it will leap to the other side. Locking the cat out of the room may lead to incessant meowing.

**WALK**

**Cats love heights.**

Get shelves for your cat to walk on so they can be up high. Their balance makes them perfect for heights. A shelf gives a cat a safe space away from a dog. Cats are confident walking high up because they have great balance and they can land on their feet if they fall. A cat has a 90% survival rate if they fall out of a five-story window.

## WATER

A cat's kidneys are so efficient they can filter water from almost anything.

**Cats can drink salt water.**

## A cat is a land shark.

It's no surprise they can drink sea water. The Turkish Van loves to swim and play in the water. Despite its name, the Turkish Van came from the United Kingdom.
Cats are descended from desert dwellers.

They get most of their water from what they eat. Cats prefer running water because it's more likely to be clean and safe. Plastic bowls can harbor bacteria and your cat can get brown spots near their mouth. Use metal bowls for water. Cats can get seventy percent of their water by eating fresh prey. Cats know when something is wrong with the water. Give them water from a different source if a cat refuses to drink.

Dry food contains no water. It should not be the main diet. It's a myth that dry food is good for their teeth. Greenies are special dental treats and are the exception. Cats like tap water that's been sitting because the chemicals have dissipated.  Don't let the water get too old because it can get bacteria. Wet food is a good source of water.

**It's a myth that cats don't like water.**

They don't like when you want to put them in it. They think you are up to no good because that's what they would do if they were bigger than you. Cats have a long history living on sailing ships. They catch mice and rats.

## WHISKERS

The whiskers tell where things are.

Whiskers are great in the dark. It will know where the shoe is that will trip you. The cat can jump over the shoe to land on you. My advice is to always leave the light on.

**Cats are farsighted.**

Cats can't see things close up. A cat loses sight of prey under its nose. Like a Venus flytrap, the whiskers trigger the grab reflex and the claws will come out and clutch its victim. Whiskers are called vibrissae and are on the legs, ears, above the eyes and on the jaw.

## WORSHIP

**Cats know they're cats.**

They also know they're cooler than you because they're a cat and you're not. Meow. Do you post pics of your cat on social media? Of course, you do. You should throw away your camera because you're only swelling your cat's head.

# YARN JITSU

**You may worship me.**

(c) Carruthers

Made in United States
North Haven, CT
26 September 2023

41984145R10153